D1523189

M. B. GOFFSTEIN

School of Names

Harper & Row, Publishers

New York

School of Names
Copyright © 1986 by M. B. Goffstein
Printed in the U.S.A. All rights reserved.

Library of Congress Cataloging-in-Publication Data
Goffstein, M. B.
  School of names.

  "A Charlotte Zolotow book."
  Summary: What it means to live on earth—to share a
connection with the ocean, the continents, the clouds,
the animals, and all elements of the earth.
  1. Science—Juvenile literature.   2. Ecology—
Juvenile literature.   [1. Earth.   2. Nature]   I. Title.
Q163.G58 1986   508   85-45419
ISBN 0-06-021984-X
ISBN 0-06-021985-8 (lib. bdg.)

Designed by Constance Fogler
1 2 3 4 5 6 7 8 9 10
First Edition

To Antonia Markiet, Constance Fogler,
and John Vitale — The Best!

I want to go
to the School of Names

to know every star
in the sky I can see
at night,
and later learn those
imagined
and proved to be there.

I want to know
what's in the ocean,
every school of fish,
every watery motion
by name.

I want to know
every stone and rock,
crystal, shale,
granite, chalk,
every kind by name.

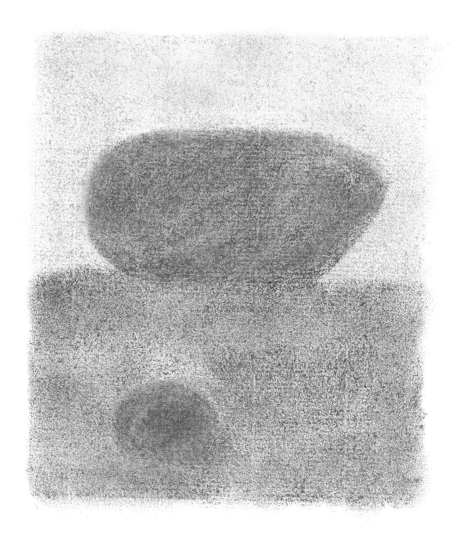

Names of the continents,

names of the seas,

names of the islands,

names of the lakes,

names of the mountains,

names of shores,

names of deserts,

names of rivers,

and the grasses, flowers,
trees, and bushes
growing on this earth.

How are the winds called?
What are the names
of clouds?

I want to go
to the School of Names

to know everybody
with me
on this globe,
every mammal, reptile,
insect,
bird, fish, and worm.

I would like
to recognize
and greet everyone
by name.

For all the years
I may live,
no place but the earth
is my home.